Countries of the World

Japan

Charles Phillips

Gil Latz and Kyohei Shibata, Consultants

NATIONAL GEOGRAPHIC
WASHINGTON, D.C.

Contents

Foreword

Japan is an ancient country. The idea that its many islands are the home of a unified nation was born more than fifteen hundred years ago and has never been challenged or threatened since. The archipelago lay at the edge of the Chinese continent, facing the vast Pacific Ocean. That made it the natural recipient of cultures, religions, and crafts that originated elsewhere in Asia and then spread east. Among other arrivals, the Japanese adopted Chinese letters, Buddhism, and Confucianism. They mingled the foreign "imports" with their own traditions to create a smart combination of sophistication and simplicity. For example, the Japanese alphabet is composed of three types: Kanji, Hiragana, and Katakana. Kanji uses Chinese characters but pronounces them differently; Hiragana and Katakana originated in Japan. The Japanese write texts using all three types of letters.

From the seventeenth century, Japan closed its islands to foreigners for more than two centuries. For Europeans and Americans, the country on the other side of the world seemed mysterious and exotic. Artists and writers found it a rich source of imagination. In the mid-19th century, however, an American fleet arrived in Japan to demand the right to trade there. Its arrival marked the moment when modern Western civilization, expanding both eastward and westward from Europe, completed its circle around the globe. Within a century, Japan transformed itself into one of the world's most dynamic economies. Over the course of the transformation, the United States, a new neighbor across the ocean, became Japan's most important partner in trade, politics, and culture—but only after a period of tension and hostility, including a bitter war.

Today, Japan is primarily known for innovative industrial products, such as automobiles and electronics. Well-known Japanese companies operate factories in many countries. Elements of Japanese culture such as food, martial arts, cartoons, and videogames are popular around the world. The ancient country is no longer simply a passive recipient of ideas. As throughout its history, however, geography will play a large part in what Japan will be for centuries to come.

▲ **Himeji Castle, built in the early seventeenth century, is one of the best-preserved symbols of the era of the shoguns, when Japan was dominated by warlords.**

Kyohei Shibata

Kyohei Shibata

Professor, Institute of Innovation Management, Graduate School of Shinshu University

Islands of
Snow
and
Sunshine

Two of Japan's best-known symbols, the high-speed bullet train and the mighty snowcapped volcano Mount Fuji, present different sides of the country. The train is sleek and modern; Fuji stands as a reminder of Japan's ancient values. But such opposites are nothing unusual; Japan is a land of many contrasts.

One cause of these contrasts is Japan's length. Its chain of almost 4,000 islands stretches 1,860 miles (2,994 km). That is about the distance from the Great Lakes to Miami, Florida. In springtime, people on the island of Okinawa in the far south can sunbathe on sandy beaches. At the same time on Hokkaido island in the north of the country, people are ice-skating outdoors and skiing in snowy mountains.

◀ **A bullet train traveling on Japan's fast and efficient railroad network passes the snow-capped Mount Fuji partially hidden by clouds.**

WHAT'S THE WEATHER LIKE?

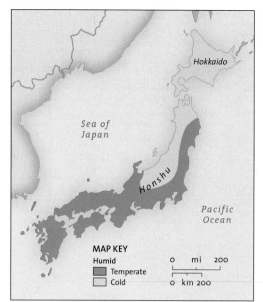

Japan's weather is usually warm but can also be very wet. The capital, Tokyo, receives up to 60 inches (152 cm) of rain a year, and rain contributes to frequent flooding. However, there are many regional variations. The northern and western coasts have very cold winters. Icy winds from Siberia bring heavy snow. The eastern and southern coasts are warmer. Winds from the Pacific keep temperatures mild but bring heavy summer rain. The map opposite shows the physical features of Japan. Labels on this map and on similar maps throughout this book identify places pictured in each chapter.

Fast Facts

OFFICIAL NAME: Japan

FORM OF GOVERNMENT: Constitutional monarchy with parliamentary government

CAPITAL: Tokyo

POPULATION: 127,463,611

OFFICIAL LANGUAGE: Japanese

MONETARY UNIT: Japanese yen

AREA: 145,883 square miles (377,835 square kilometers)

HIGHEST POINT: Mount Fuji 12,388 feet (3,776 meters)

LOWEST POINT: Hachiro-gata −13 feet (−4 meters)

MAJOR RIVERS: Ishikari, Kitakami, Shinano, Tone

MAJOR LAKES: Biwa, Inawashiro, Kasumigaura

Average Temperature & Rainfall

Average High/Low Temperatures; Yearly Rainfall

Sapporo (Hokkaido island)
72° F (22° C) / 24° F (−4° C); 43 in (110 cm)

Akita (Honshu island)
77° F (25° C) / 31° F (0° C); 70 in (179 cm)

Tokyo (Honshu island)
81° F (27° C) / 44° F (6° C); 60 in (152 cm)

Osaka (Honshu island)
84° F (29° C) / 42° F (5° C); 53 in (135 cm)

Fukuoka (Kyushu island)
83° F (28° C) / 44° F (6° C); 64 in (163 cm)

Naha (Okinawa island)
84° F (29° C) / 61° F (16° C); 83 in (210cm)

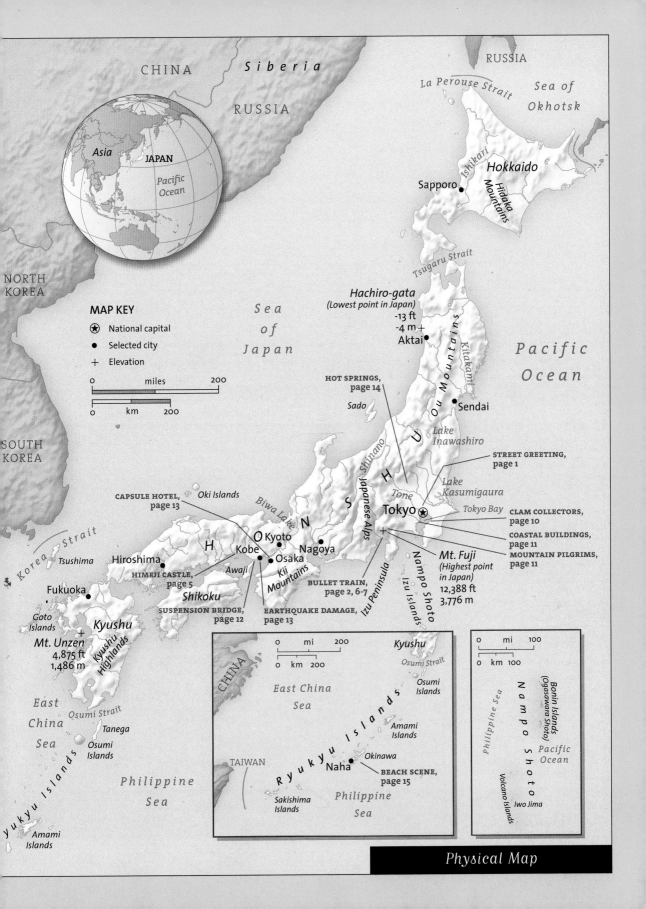

CHINA

Siberia

RUSSIA

RUSSIA

La Perouse Strait

*Sea of
Okhotsk*

Asia   **JAPAN**

*Pacific
Ocean*

NORTH
KOREA

Hokkaido

Sapporo

Hidaka
Mountains

Ishikari

SOUTH
KOREA

Tsugaru Strait

Hachiro-gata
(Lowest point in Japan)
-13 ft
-4 m ✛
Aktai

*Sea
of
Japan*

MAP KEY

⊛ National capital

● Selected city

✛ Elevation

Kitakami

*Pacific
Ocean*

0   miles   200

0   km   200

HOT SPRINGS,
page 14

Sado

Sendai

O
u
Mountains

*Lake
Inawashiro*

STREET GREETING,
page 1

Shinano

CAPSULE HOTEL,
page 13

Oki Islands

Biwa Lake

Japanese Alps

N

S

*Lake
Kasumigaura*

H

Tokyo ⊛

Tokyo Bay

CLAM COLLECTORS,
page 10

Tone

H

O   Kyoto

Kobe

Nagoya

COASTAL BUILDINGS,
page 11

Hiroshima

HIMEJI CASTLE,
page 5

Awaji

Osaka

Kii
Mountains

MOUNTAIN PILGRIMS,
page 11

✛

Nampo Shoto
Izu Islands

Mt. Fuji
(Highest point
in Japan)
12,388 ft
3,776 m

Korea

Strait

Tsushima

Shikoku

BULLET TRAIN,
page 2, 6-7

Izu Peninsula

Fukuoka

SUSPENSION BRIDGE,
page 12

EARTHQUAKE DAMAGE,
page 13

*Goto
Islands*

Kyushu

✛
Mt. Unzen
4,875 ft
1,486 m

Kyushu
Highlands

*East
China
Sea*

Osumi Strait

Tanega

*Osumi
Islands*

0   mi   200

Kyushu

0   km   200

CHINA

Osumi Strait

*East China
Sea*

*Osumi
Islands*

0   mi   100

0   km   100

yukyu Islands

*Amami
Islands*

TAIWAN

Ryukyu Islands

*Amami
Islands*

Naha

Okinawa

BEACH SCENE,
page 15

*Philippine
Sea*

*Sakishima
Islands*

*Philippine
Sea*

Philippine Sea

Nampo Shoto

*Bonin Islands
(Ogasawara Shoto)*

*Pacific
Ocean*

Volcano Islands

Iwo Jima

Physical Map

Mountainous Land of Beauty

The Japanese people have a deep affection for the beauty of the landscape. According to the ancient religion of Shinto, which most Japanese observe, natural features such as mountains, waterfalls, and forests possess their own spirits, like souls, called *kami*.

Almost four-fifths of Japan is covered by mountains. The tallest peaks lie in the Japanese Alps, which run down the center of the largest island, Honshu. Japan's highest mountain, however, is Mount Fuji, which many Japanese consider sacred.

The mountains limit the amount of space for building outside the cities, where most of Japan's 127 million people live. City-dwellers often take a break in the hills or by the coast. The country is so narrow that everyone can travel to the beach in a couple of hours.

► The beach is a popular place to relax in Japan. This one has an extra attraction: clams. For a small fee, visitors can collect a feast of delicious shellfish at low tide.

JAPAN'S SACRED MOUNTAIN

On a clear day, workers in Tokyo can look to the west and see snowcapped Mount Fuji, just 60 miles (97 km) away. The mountain is revered for its sacred meaning and beauty. The Japanese see it as a symbol of their country's unique traditions.

Since the 15th century, followers of the Shinto and Buddhist faiths have climbed Mount Fuji to pray at the summit. Each year, 250,000 people climb the mountain; religious pilgrims join tourists from Japan and around the world to make the climb. The official climbing season falls in July and August, when the weather is good for clear views.

Climbers in winter sometimes die of exposure. Shinto pilgrims climb in white robes to honor the sun goddess Amaterasu. Japanese Buddhists believe that the Buddha of All-Illuminating Wisdom, Dainichi Nyorai, dwells at the summit.

A String of Islands

Japan is an archipelago, or string of islands. There are four main islands. Hokkaido is the farthest north. Next comes Honshu, which is bigger than the other three islands combined and is where much of Japan's industry is based. The dynamic capital city, Tokyo, lies on the eastern coast of Honshu. To the south are the islands of Shikoku and then Kyushu.

Japan is also made up of 3,918 smaller islands, some of which are barely larger than

▼ Bridges and causeways, like these at the edge of Tokyo Bay, help make the most of land available for building along the coast.

COMMUTERS IN SUSPENSE

The Akashi-Kaikyo Bridge, the longest suspension bridge in the world, stretches 2.43 miles (3.9 km) across the Akashi Strait between the cities of Kobe in south-central Honshu and Iwaya on Awaji Island. It also has the tallest towers—928 feet (282 m)—of any bridge. The bridge, which is more than twice as long as the Brooklyn Bridge in New York City, cost 500 billion yen ($5 billion) to build.

Around 150,000 people live on Awaji, many of whom work in Honshu. Commuters used to cross the strait by boat, but in 1955 two ferries sank in a storm, drowning 168 children. The authorities decided to build a bridge, but it took decades to plan and raise money for the project. Work began in 1988; the bridge finally opened in 1998.

The bridge is designed to withstand earthquakes, which are common in Japan. Its strength was tested while it was being built, when it survived the Kobe earthquake in 1995. It can also withstand winds of 178 miles per hour (286 km/h). The bridge is lit up at night, and colorful patterns are projected onto it during public holidays.

rocks. In the seas south of Kyushu lie the Ryukyu Islands, of which Okinawa is the largest. The Ogasawara Islands, southeast of Honshu, stretch 1,200 miles (1,930 km) into the Pacific. The islands count as part of Tokyo, even though the islanders may never have seen the city.

Japan lies along the eastern edge of Asia. Its nearest mainland neighbors across the Sea of Japan are the Siberian region of Russia in the north and Korea and China farther south. East of Japan, the vast Pacific Ocean stretches to North America.

The warm Tsushima Current flows from the south into the Sea of Japan, where it meets a colder current from the north. The mixing waters make the seas around Japan very rich in fish and other sea life.

▲ Earthquake damage in Kobe in 1995. Although many of Japan's new buildings are designed to withstand earthquakes, older homes and buildings may collapse during major tremors.

Land of Danger

Japan can be a dangerous place. Three of the plates that form the Earth's crust meet nearby and often move against one another, causing earthquakes. More than a thousand earthquakes hit Japan every year. When the tremors occur under the seabed, the vibrations may create a tsunami or tidal wave. *Tsunami* is a Japanese word.

IT'S A SQUEEZE

Three-quarters of Japan's 127 million people live in towns and cities where there is very little space. Most families live in apartments with just one room for cooking, eating, and relaxing. Japanese cities cover huge areas, and it is common for people to travel two hours to get to work. Then they may work a ten-hour day or more. "Capsule" hotels offer tiny rooms to commuters who have missed the last train home.

▲ The rooms at a capsule hotel are just large enough to lie down in.

The most serious Japanese earthquake of the 20th century hit Tokyo on September 1, 1923. Around 140,000 people died. A large quake struck Kobe on Honshu in 1995. It killed more than 5,000 people.

Another danger comes from volcanoes. Japan has around 200 volcanoes, 60 of which are active. They include Mount Fuji, although it has not erupted since 1707. The origin of Fuji's name is a mystery. One theory is that it means "without equal." Japan's most serious recent eruption was that of Mount Unzen on Kyushu in 1991.

The Japanese also have to look out for typhoons—the name given to hurricanes in the Pacific. The word *typhoon* comes from the Japanese *taifu*. The typhoon season lasts from June to October each year. Storms make landfall along the western or eastern coasts and cause millions of yen in damage.

▲ One benefit of the geothermal activity that causes earthquakes and volcanoes is hot springs, which make popular bathing resorts like this one on Honshu.

The Frozen North

Hokkaido takes up 20 percent of Japan's land area, but is home to just 5 percent of its people. The island has heavy snows and popular ski resorts. The largest city, Sapporo, hosted the Winter Olympics in 1972. Today it holds a snow festival each February. Artists from around the world carve elaborate ice sculptures.

Ancient and Modern

On Honshu, too, the mountainous north and west can be bitterly cold. The Japanese call the region facing the Sea of Japan "the Snow Coast," and few people live there. In contrast, the eastern coast is crowded. Three cities—Tokyo, Yokohama, and Osaka—are home to 14.5 million Japanese.

Japan's oldest cities are in south-central Honshu. They include Kyoto, which has many shrines related to Shinto and temples related to Japan's other major religion, Buddhism.

▲ A father and son relax on a beach on Okinawa. The island was governed by the United States after World War II ended in 1945, but again became part of Japan in 1972.

Tropical Islands

South of Shikoku and Kyushu lie smaller islands. Many, such as Okinawa and Iwo Jima, are located far out in the ocean. People call Okinawa the "Hawaii of Japan." Vacationers flock there to enjoy the beaches of white sand, glistening blue sea, and spectacular coral reefs.

Living
with
Nature

The Japanese people have a great respect for nature. However, most Japanese live in cities, where there is little room for open spaces or backyards. Some have adapted Japanese traditions to fit the crowded urban environment. They construct small gardens of stones and gravel to reflect the shape of entire landscapes. People also expertly prune regular trees using the art of bonsai. The results look just like full-size trees, but are still small enough to keep in a pot.

Cities cover less than 10 percent of Japan's land. City-dwellers like to spend time away from home in the mountains or by the coast. One popular destination is the Izu peninsula, south of Tokyo, where people scuba dive in the Pacific Ocean or relax in hot springs.

◀ **A bonsai tree is transported through the grounds of the emperor's palace in Tokyo. The tree is decades old, but it is barely taller than the gardeners.**

BEAUTIFUL GARDENS

The Japanese love to admire the beauty of natural forms, such as the shape of a tree or rock, or the course of a stream. They attempt to re-create that beauty in their gardens. With little space to spare, Japanese gardens are often very small. They are made following a set of rules that makes each garden quiet and soothing. Some gardens have no plants at all. Instead, rocks and gravel are used to represent an idealized version of the natural world.

The map opposite shows the vegetation zones—or what grows where—in Japan. Each zone supports certain types of wildlife. A long country with a varied climate, Japan has a wide range of vegetation zones.

▶ **A gardener tends a restful Japanese garden, raking gravel into a pattern.**

Species at Risk

Most of Japan is covered by countryside, but such a high number of people living in such a small country has inevitably impacted wildlife. Although pollution is now tightly controlled, human activity such as road building has damaged natural habitats. No fewer than 136 species living in or around Japan are listed as endangered. The following are some of the species at risk:

> Amami rabbit
> Amami thrush
> Asiatic black bear
> Blue whale
> Bonin fruit bat
> Bonin honeyeater (bird)
> Bonin white eye (bird)
> Echigo mole
> Fin whale
> Gloomy tube-nosed bat
> Humpback whale
> Iriomote wildcat

> Izu thrush
> Japanese dormouse
> Japanese macaque
> Marianas flying fox
> Muenk's spiny rat
> Northern fur seal
> Okinawa rail (bird)
> Okinawa woodpecker
> Ryukyu mole
> Sea otter
> Steller sea lion
> Yellow bunting (bird)

CHINA

RUSSIA

Sea of Okhotsk

La Perouse Strait

BEAR CUBS,
page 20

Hokkaido

Akan
N.P.

● Sapporo

Ishikari

*Daisetsuzan
N.P.*

NORTH
KOREA

Tsugaru Strait

MAP KEY

**Primary Vegetation
Zones/Ecosystems**

Tropical broadleaf forest

Temperate broadleaf forest

Temperate coniferous forest

**Protected
Lands**

National park

Other protected land

*Sea
of
Japan*

Ou Mountains

● Sendai

*Pacific
Ocean*

SOUTH
KOREA

Sado

SNOW MONKEYS,
page 21

*Joshinetsu
Kogen N.P.*

TEMPLE GARDEN,
page 18

Oki Islands

*Chubu
Sangaku N.P.*

CHERRY BLOSSOM
PARTY,
page 22

*Lake
Biwa*

H O N S H U

Japanese Alps

Tone

★ Tokyo

IMPERIAL PALACE
GARDENS,
pages 2, 16-17

Korea Strait

Hiroshima ●

Kobe ●

● Kyoto

● Nagoya

● Yokohama

Osaka ●

Fuji-Hakone-
Izu N.P.

Fukuoka ●

Shikoku

*Yoshino-
Kumano N.P.*

*Izu
Islands*

Kyushu

*Kyushu
Highlands*

*Philippine
Sea*

*East
China
Sea*

Osumi Strait

*Osumi
Islands*

yukyu Islands

*Amami
Islands*

0   miles   200

0   km   200

Kyushu

0   mi   200

0   km   200

CHINA

*East China
Sea*

*Osumi
Islands*

TAIWAN

*Amami
Islands*

R y u k y u   I s l a n d s

Okinawa

*Iriomote
N.P.*

*Sakishima
Islands*

*Philippine
Sea*

Vegetation & Ecosystems Map

Fir Trees and Heavy Snow

The largest rural area in Japan is on Hokkaido, in the far north. People travel there to admire the rugged mountains, lakes, and thick forests. Seven of Japan's 27 national parks are located on this island.

Hokkaido is close to Siberia, a vast, icy region of northern Asia. Winds from Siberia make the island's climate very cold, with heavy snowfall. Snow often lies on the ground for six months of the year. The average winter temperature is 24° F (−4° C). In some inland areas, it drops as low as −22° F (−30° C) in winter.

Animals and plants have adapted to the cold temperatures. The forests of Hokkaido are filled with firs and other trees with needlelike leaves that do not lose their heat. The animals include snow monkeys, or macaques, and brown bears. The snow monkeys have much thicker fur than those that live farther south, and the bears are twice as big as those that live elsewhere in Japan. Such big bodies are good at keeping heat in, because their surface area is quite small compared to their size, so there is less area to lose heat from.

▼ These brown bear cubs are being looked after in a home in Hokkaido. The native Ainu people of Hokkaido believe that they descended from bears, which they worship.

Broadleaf Forests

The wildlife on the three other main islands—Honshu, Shikoku, and Kyushu—is similar to that found in the northeastern United States and Europe.

THE SNOW MONKEY

Fiercely cold winters in the snowy forests of Hokkaido and Honshu do not bother the Japanese macaque. No other species of monkey lives so far north and in such cold conditions. The macaques, also known as snow monkeys, survive in temperatures as low as 5° F (-15° C). Some monkeys have learned to keep warm by sitting in hot pools formed by volcanic springs. Others head south to avoid the worst of the cold; the species is found in all parts of Japan.

Snow monkeys have bright red faces and a thick blanket of fur, which turns pale gray in winter. The monkeys survive by eating bark and fir cones. In spring, their fur darkens to brown and begins to thin as the weather becomes warmer. Monkeys are often featured in Japan's folk tales. Today, the animals' survival is under threat because their forest homes are being polluted or destroyed. There are thought to be only about 35,000 macaques left in the wild.

Animals living on the islands include wild boars, ferrets, and black bears. There are also animals known as *tanuki* in Japanese. These animals look like raccoons but are small relatives of foxes. Among the many birds are hawks, cranes, ducks, and pheasants.

Almost 60 percent of Japan's land is covered with forests of broadleaf trees—with wide and flat leaves—such as chestnut, oak, and beech. In central and southern Japan, plum and cherry trees flower with beautiful blossoms in spring.

▲ A hanami party beneath a cherry tree on the island of Kyushu.

CHERRY BLOSSOMS

Every spring the Japanese hold *hanami* parties to celebrate the appearance of beautiful pink and white blossoms on cherry trees. They get together and picnic beneath the trees. The trees in the warm south of Japan blossom before those in the colder areas farther north.

Most varieties of cherry tree bloom for only a few days. The television news carries reports on the best places to see them bloom. People watch excitedly as the bloom "moves" north each year. They call the movement the "cherry-blossom front." Because the blooms die so quickly after they appear, people feel a mixture of pleasure and sadness at the hanami parties. The cherry blossom reminds the Japanese of an important teaching of the Buddhist religion: that life is temporary.

Throughout spring and summer, Japan's nature lovers look out for irises, the beautiful white flowers of hydrangea bushes, and the bright blooms of azalea shrubs. In fall, they admire the colors of red maple trees and chrysanthemums—known as *kiku*. Magnolia and Japanese cedar trees are popular in gardens.

Tropical Islands

The chains of islands that form the far south of Japan lie close to the tropics, the part of the Earth near the equator, an imaginary line that runs around the middle of the globe. This part of the Japanese archipelago is warm all year around; it is often also very wet. Japan's subtropical islands are regularly hit by typhoons and other storms that bring heavy rains.

The southern Ryukyu Islands, which run through the East China Sea, are soaked by monsoons—downpours caused by a seasonal change in wind direction. As a result, Japan's southern islands are covered in lush forests made up of palms and mangroves, which are home to spectacular wild orchids and hundreds of other tropical flowers.

Rare Species

All islands are cut off from other land by the ocean, and remote islands might have remained undisturbed by the outside world for millions of years. As a result, islands are home to some of the world's rarest plants and animals. The Ogasawara Islands southeast of Honshu are a treasure trove of rare species. There are more than 250 plants and several species of animals there that exist nowhere else. Among them are the Bonin honeyeater, the Japanese wood pigeon, and the very rare Bonin fruit bat.

The rarest species in Japan—the Iriomote wildcat—lives on just one island at the southern tip of the Ryukyu Islands, barely 50 miles (80 km) from Taiwan. The wildcat was discovered only in 1965. With just 100 animals left, the species is the rarest cat in the world.

▼ **This painted screen from the 16th century shows chrysanthemums. The flower is a national symbol: the Japanese monarchy is known as the "Chrysanthemum Throne."**

Emperors
and
Samurai

The samurai dominated Japan from the 1100s to the 1800s. Skilled horsemen and outstanding swordfighters, these warriors lived by a code called Bushido, which valued courage, honor, and loyalty. Even in the first half of the 20th century (1900–1950), the Japanese army was still being trained according to Bushido. In the 1930s, society as a whole was dominated by militaristic discipline.

Since World War II ended in 1945, Japan has changed enormously. It has reemerged as a major economic power. The samurai and the strict system of social class to which they belonged passed into history in the nineteenth century. Today they feature only in movies, in reenactments of their battles, or in exhibits in the impressive castles the samurai built across Japan.

◀ **Dressed in samurai armor, a young man shops after taking part in a festival commemorating a historical event. The Japanese are proud of their long history.**

FIRST FARMERS

People first came to Japan about 30,000 years ago, at the end of the last Ice Age. The main islands of Japan were then connected to Siberia and Korea by bridges of dry land, and the first Japanese crossed on foot.

The first society in Japan emerged about 12,000 years ago. Historians call the culture Jomon (meaning "straw rope") because they pressed straw rope into wet clay to make marks on their pots.

Around the same time, the Ainu arrived by boat from Siberia—the sea level had risen as the ice melted, and the land bridges had disappeared. Today the Ainu live only in Hokkaido, in northern Japan. Unlike other Japanese, the Ainu have round eyes and pale skin.

The Jomon and the Ainu lived in Japan for thousands of years. They survived by fishing, hunting, and gathering plants. In 300 B.C. another group of people, the Yayoi, began to move onto Japan's largest island, Honshu, from Korea and China. They were skilled at weaving and could make weapons and tools in bronze and iron. They were also skilled farmers—they knew how to grow rice in flooded paddy fields.

▲ The Ainu of Hokkaido are struggling to keep their traditions, costume, and dance alive in modern Japan.

Time line

The chart shows the approximate dates of some of the major periods of Japanese history. The country was unified under imperial rule beginning about A.D. 350.

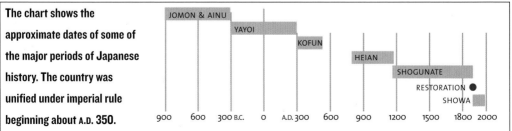

JOMON & AINU

YAYOI

KOFUN

HEIAN

SHOGUNATE

RESTORATION ●

SHOWA

900   600   300 B.C.   0   A.D. 300   600   900   1200   1500   1800 2000

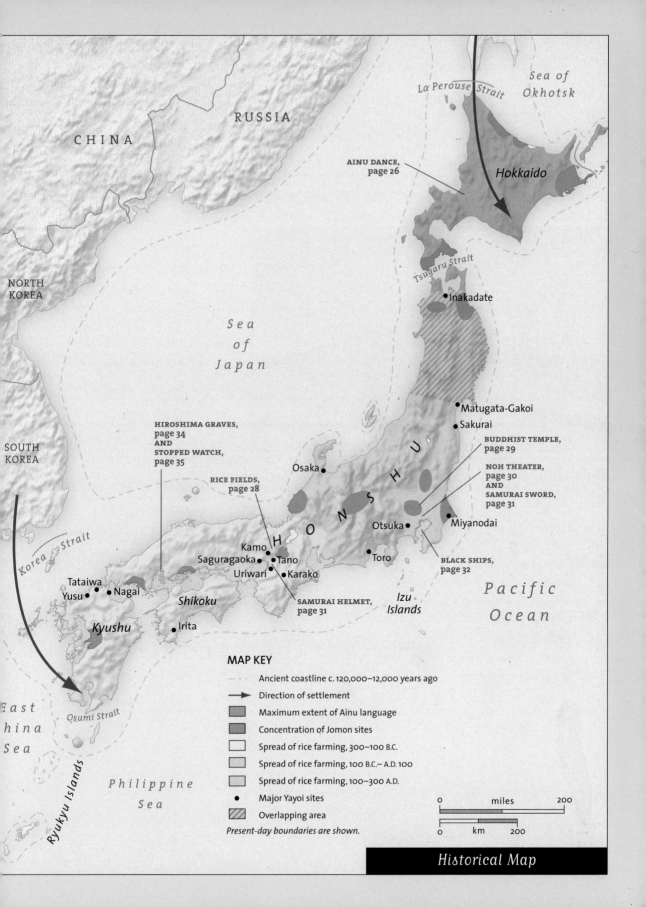

RUSSIA

CHINA

*Sea of
Okhotsk*

La Perouse Strait

AINU DANCE,
page 26

Hokkaido

NORTH
KOREA

Tsugaru Strait

•Inakadate

*Sea
of
Japan*

HIROSHIMA GRAVES,
page 34
AND
STOPPED WATCH,
page 35

•Matugata-Gakoi

•Sakurai

SOUTH
KOREA

RICE FIELDS,
page 28

Osaka•

BUDDHIST TEMPLE,
page 29

NOH THEATER,
page 30
AND
SAMURAI SWORD,
page 31

H   O   N   S   H   U

Korea Strait

Kamo•
Saguragaoka• •Tano
Uriwari• •Karako

Otsuka•

•Miyanodai

Toro•

BLACK SHIPS,
page 32

Tataiwa•
Yusu• •Nagai

Shikoku

SAMURAI HELMET,
page 31

*Izu
Islands*

*Pacific
Ocean*

Kyushu

•Irita

MAP KEY

*East
China
Sea*

Osumi Strait

– – – Ancient coastline c. 120,000–12,000 years ago

→ Direction of settlement

Maximum extent of Ainu language

Concentration of Jomon sites

Spread of rice farming, 300–100 B.C.

Spread of rice farming, 100 B.C.– A.D. 100

Spread of rice farming, 100–300 A.D.

• Major Yayoi sites

Overlapping area

Ryukyu Islands

*Philippine
Sea*

Present-day boundaries are shown.

0   miles   200

0   km   200

Historical Map

The Divine Emperor

Early Japan was divided into local areas, each ruled by a clan or tribe. Sometimes one clan took control of others. In about A.D. 400, the Yamato from near Osaka became the most powerful clan in Japan.

The Yamato clan worshiped Amaterasu, the Shinto sun goddess. The clan's ruler acted as her high priest. Later, the Yamato ruler was declared emperor of Japan and was said to be a relative of the sun goddess. According to legend, the first emperor, Jimmu Tenno ("Divine Soldier"), was Amaterasu's grandson. He had come to the throne in 660 B.C., when the goddess gave him a sword, mirror, and jeweled necklace as a sign of her favor. When Japanese emperors are crowned today, they are still given the same symbols of power as in the legend of the first emperor.

▲ The practice of growing rice in wet-paddy fields reached Japan around 300 B.C., possibly from China. It allowed farmers to grow more food, so other people could stop working on the land and do a wider range of work.

Ideas from China and Korea

The Yamato clan was heavily influenced by ideas from Korea and China. The first books in Japan, which arrived in A.D. 392, were written in Chinese. The Japanese learned to use Chinese symbols or ideograms to write their own language. The Buddhist religion also arrived from China, in 552. The faith had spread from India, where it was based on the teachings of a Nepalese prince from the fifth century B.C., known as the Buddha. He said that people's suffering comes from them wanting things, and that they could learn to overcome ignorance and sorrow.

The ideas of the Chinese thinker Confucius (551–479 B.C.) reached Japan in the 600s. Confucianism—a code that encouraged people to be respectful, generous, and loyal—had great influence on Japanese behavior. It urged people to be loyal to local leaders and to the emperor. Today, Confucianism still influences social relationships in Japan.

A Buddhist Country

A clan named the Soga won power in Japan in the sixth century and made Buddhism the official religion. The Soga were overthrown about 100 years later. A

▼ Novice monks follow a lesson at a Zen Buddhist temple. Zen Buddhism emphasizes the importance of meditation and self-discipline. It was important to the samurai and to other parts of Japanese culture.

new emperor, Tenji, then reorganized Japan. He created a central government along Chinese lines and decreed that all land now belonged to the emperor—the country's divine leader.

In 710, a new capital city, Heijo, was built on the site of modern Nara. A network of roads connected the capital to the provinces. Emperor Shomu, who ruled from 724 to 749, built Buddhist temples and monasteries in every province.

After Shomu's death, the Fujiwara clan dominated Japan for four centuries, from 750 to 1155. They built another new capital, at Heian (modern Kyoto).

▲ Actors from a Noh theater dress a cast member as a samurai. The shoguns granted the samurai privileges in return for their support, but later tried to limit their power.

The Shoguns Take Power

By the 12th century, the Fujiwara had lost control of the country. Regional rulers fought each other for political power. After a fierce war among rival groups, the Minamoto clan took military control. A new emperor was crowned, but the real power lay with the clan's military leader, Minamoto Yoritomo. He took the title *shogun*, meaning "imperial general."

Under the shogun's rule, the emperor had no real political power. He became a godlike figurehead.

Japan's provinces were governed instead by soldiers appointed by the shogun. Each governor's authority came from the loyalty of his samurai warriors.

Europeans Arrive

Japan flourished under the stability created by the rule of shoguns. The country was peaceful. However, by about 1450, the shogun's grip on the country was weakening. Warlords, local rulers with their own military forces, broke away from the shogun and began to rule areas of the country as their own.

▲ Craftsmen spent months making the blades of samurai swords fine enough to cut almost anything.

JAPAN'S WARRIOR KNIGHTS

Beginning in the mid-1100s, when Japan was first ruled by shoguns, samurai warriors were members of an elite. They followed a set of rules called Bushido, or "the way of the warrior." According to Bushido, a samurai should be willing to give his life to win victory for his clan. If he shamed his clan, he should kill himself by *hari-kiri*—cutting open his own stomach. Samurai trained at archery, martial arts, and sword fighting. They adopted Zen Buddhism, which strengthened concentration through meditation and self-discipline. Many famous stories about samurai are based on the struggle between the Minamoto and their rivals in the 1100s. For the next 650 years, the samurai were the most powerful people in Japan, before they began to lose their importance.

▶ Samurai helmets, often adorned with fierce masks, gave protection against blows to the back of the neck.

A COMMODORE VISITS

When U.S. commodore Matthew C. Perry (1794–1858) sailed into Edo Bay in July 1853, the Japanese called his vessels "black ships," because they were painted with tar. The steamships were a sign of how far Japan had fallen behind the West in its industry and power. After Perry's show of strength, the Japanese signed trade agreements with the United States. Many Japanese also concluded that the country needed to modernize. The need for change eventually triggered the end of the shogunate in 1868.

▶ An illustration in Japanese style shows a scholar rowing out to meet the American ships.

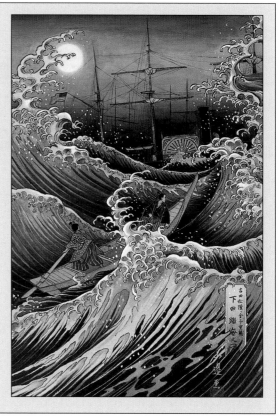

That was still the case when sailors from Portugal landed in Kyushu in 1543. They were the first Europeans to visit Japan. The sailors brought guns with them, which changed fighting in Japan forever. Christian missionaries brought yet more changes. Within 50 years, 150,000 Japanese had become Christians.

Closing the Country

Various warlords tried to win control of Japan. One, named Oda Nobunaga, was the first Japanese leader to make wide use of guns in his army. He united the country briefly in the 1570s. In 1600 another warlord,

Tokugawa Ieyasu, declared himself ruler. He based his shogunate at Edo, which later became Tokyo.

Ieyasu's successors, the Tokugawa shoguns, chose to cut Japan off from the outside world. In 1635, they banned Japanese from traveling abroad. Four years later they forced all non-Japanese to leave. The only exceptions were a few Chinese traders and Dutch merchants, who were allowed to dock once a year at a small island near Nagasaki.

Japan's isolation lasted until 1858, when the Japanese signed a trade agreement with the United States.

Meiji Modernization

By this stage the Tokugawa shoguns did not have much authority. In 1868, their government was overthrown by clans from southwest Japan, who restored rule by the emperor. The 15-year-old Emperor Mutsuhito moved his government to Edo, which was renamed Tokyo ("Eastern Capital"). The new age was called Meiji ("Enlightened Rule").

The Meiji era was a time of great change. The new government swept away the social system that had made the samurai so important. It encouraged industrial development, and Japan caught up with the West, building railroads and manufacturing iron and steel on a large scale.

▲ Mutsuhito (1852–1912), the Meiji Emperor, led Japan's development into a modern nation. Under his reign, Japan became the first Asian country to defeat a Western state in modern warfare, when it defeated Russia in 1905.

At the same time as introducing new things, the government emphasized Japan's ancient traditions. The old faith of Shinto was made the official religion in 1872. The myths about Shinto gods and goddesses were taught in schools as if they were historical fact.

World Wars

By the eve of World War I, Japan was the dominant military power in East Asia, having won wars against both China and Russia. Japan fought in World War I (1914–1918) on the side of the United States, Great Britain, and their allies. In the 1930s, the military became powerful in politics. They wanted Japan to build an empire. In 1941, the military took control of Japan's government.

Japan clashed with the United States over trade. It launched a surprise attack on the U.S. Navy base at Pearl Harbor, Hawaii, on December 7, 1941. Japan then joined Germany and Italy to fight against Britain, Russia, and the United States in World War II (1941–1945).

The Japanese were skilled fighters and soon took control of Southeast Asia. The U.S. Navy won a crucial naval victory at Midway in June 1942 that halted Japan's advance, however. U.S. forces fought their way from island to island across the Pacific

▼ **Decorated graves of some of the victims of the Hiroshima bomb.**

toward Japan. Japanese soldiers had been taught not to surrender. Hundreds of thousands of troops and civilians died resisting the U.S. advance. It seemed that an Allied invasion of Japan itself might cost millions of Allied and Japanese lives.

◀ A watch stopped by the blast at 8:16 A.M., the moment the atom bomb exploded at Hiroshima on August 6, 1945.

To force Japan to surrender, the U.S. Air Force dropped an atomic bomb on Hiroshima on August 6, 1945. It destroyed the city, killing 150,000 people. A second bomb on August 9 struck Nagasaki. Around 115,000 people died. Japan surrendered a few days later.

Recovery after the War

Allied forces, largely American, occupied Japan until 1952. They brought in a constitution based on American democracy. Japanese women got the right to vote for the first time.

▼ Japan's current emperor is Akihito, who succeeded his father, Hirohito, in 1989. The modern emperor and empress are figureheads. Japan is now governed by a prime minister.

In the years after the war, Japan became a great industrial nation. It was famous as an innovator, making cameras, cars, and high-tech electronics. Today, Japan is a leading economic power. But most Japanese combine their modern lives with their old traditions: the ceremonies of Buddhism or the 2,000-year-old Shinto religion.

A New Start for the New Year

Just before midnight on December 31, large bells ring out 108 times from temples across Japan. As they chime, people hope for good fortune in the New Year. The following day they will make a new start.

New Year, or Shogatsu, is the most important Japanese holiday. Families celebrate together for the first three days of January. Children receive gifts of money called "New Year Treasure," and adults exchange presents. On New Year's morning, families eat a breakfast of rice cakes and chicken soup. Then they visit friends and go to shrines to pray for success in the new year. Many thousands visit Tokyo's Meiji Shrine over the holiday. The shrine honors Emperor Mutsuhito, the founder of modern Japan.

◀ At new year, visitors to a shrine tie pieces of paper to a fence. The notes, which predict people's fortunes for the coming year, are left to ask for the gods' protection.

A CROWDED PLACE

Japan is 25 times smaller than the United States, with an area slightly less than that of California. But its population of around 127 million is the tenth largest of any country in the world.

Japan's cities are especially crowded because 80 percent of the country is mountainous or forested, with few people. The Pacific coast of Honshu, the largest island, has large plains. Many of Japan's cities are located there, partly for historical reasons, but also because the land is suitable for building.

Japan's people are also getting older. The average age is rising more quickly than anywhere else in the world apart from Italy. In 1955, only one in every 20 Japanese people was over 65. Today the figure is one in five.

Common Japanese Phrases

Here are a few words and phrases you might use in Japan. Give them a try:

Ohaiyou Gozaimasu (oh-hah-YOH go-zigh-moss) Good morning

Konichiwa (koh-nee-chee-WAH) Good afternoon

Konbanwa (komh-bann-WAH) Good evening

Moshi-moshi (MO-sh-ee, mosh-ee) Hello (when answering the telephone)

Sayonara (sa-YOH-nah-rah) Goodbye

Ja-ne (JAH-nay) See you!

Domo (DOH-moh) Thank you

Yokoso (YO-ko-soh) Welcome!

▲ People pushers, or *oshiya*, help passengers safely onto Tokyo's crowded subway trains.

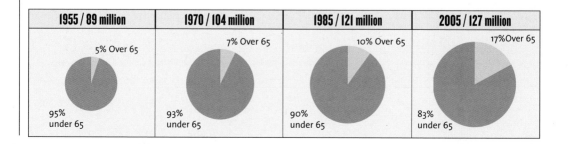

1955 / 89 million	1970 / 104 million	1985 / 121 million	2005 / 127 million
5% Over 65	7% Over 65	10% Over 65	17% Over 65
95% under 65	93% under 65	90% under 65	83% under 65

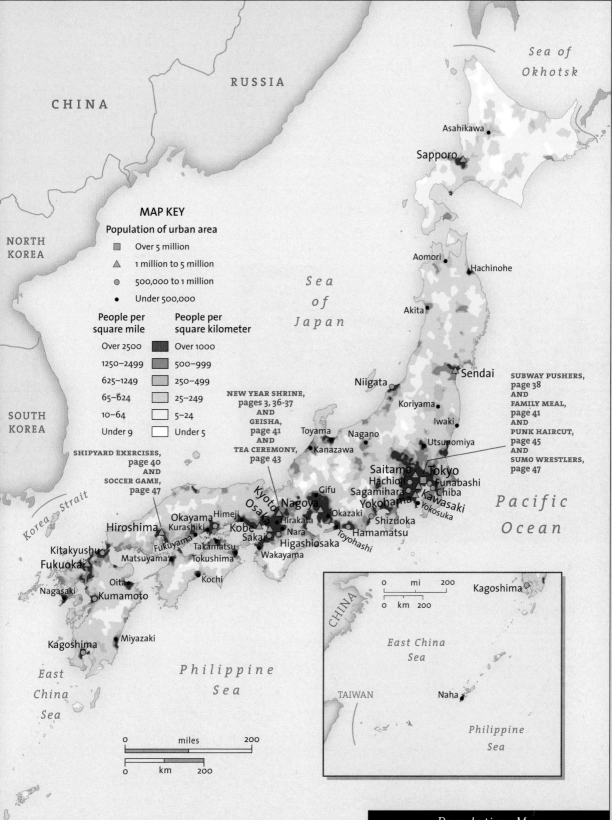

MAP KEY

Population of urban area

■ Over 5 million

▲ 1 million to 5 million

● 500,000 to 1 million

• Under 500,000

People per square mile	People per square kilometer
Over 2500	Over 1000
1250–2499	500–999
625–1249	250–499
65–624	25–249
10–64	5–24
Under 9	Under 5

NEW YEAR SHRINE,
pages 3, 36-37
AND
GEISHA,
page 41
AND
TEA CEREMONY,
page 43

SHIPYARD EXERCISES,
page 40
AND
SOCCER GAME,
page 47

SUBWAY PUSHERS,
page 38
AND
FAMILY MEAL,
page 41
AND
PUNK HAIRCUT,
page 45
AND
SUMO WRESTLERS,
page 47

RUSSIA

CHINA

NORTH KOREA

SOUTH KOREA

Korea Strait

Sea of Okhotsk

Sea of Japan

Pacific Ocean

East China Sea

Philippine Sea

Asahikawa

Sapporo

Aomori

Hachinohe

Akita

Niigata

Sendai

Koriyama

Iwaki

Utsunomiya

Toyama

Nagano

Kanazawa

Saitama

Tokyo

Hachioji

Funabashi

Sagamihara

Chiba

Yokohama

Kawasaki

Yokosuka

Gifu

Okazaki

Shizuoka

Hamamatsu

Kyoto

Osaka

Nagoya

Himeji

Hirakata

Kobe

Nara

Toyohashi

Sakai

Higashiosaka

Okayama

Kurashiki

Fukuyama

Takamatsu

Tokushima

Wakayama

Hiroshima

Matsuyama

Kochi

Kitakyushu

Fukuoka

Oita

Nagasaki

Kumamoto

Kagoshima

Miyazaki

East China Sea

CHINA

TAIWAN

Kagoshima

Naha

East China Sea

Philippine Sea

0	mi	200
0	km	200

0	miles	200
0	km	200

Population Map

Salarymen and Office Ladies

The Japanese are famous for their willingness to work very hard. "Salarymen," or male office workers, work long hours, sometimes six days a week. Many leave home before their children are up and get back after they are in bed in the evening. Salarymen may commute for two hours or more from the suburbs to their offices in the city centers. After work, many men are expected to socialize with their colleagues before

making the journey home. Women such as secretaries and clerks, known as "office ladies," also work long hours. However, many other women start their own firms, or do jobs where they can set their own hours.

In the past, Japanese people stayed in one job until they retired at age 60. That began to change in the 1990s, when the economy started to struggle. Today, many younger Japanese workers change jobs regularly.

People in Japan are taught to show respect for others, especially their parents and bosses. Respect is a key teaching of Confucianism, which many Japanese follow. People learn to do what is best for their family

▲ Shipyard workers exercise at the start of the day. Many offices and factories encourage group activities—some even have a company song for employees to sing.

and company, and to worry less about their own needs. In business meetings, people try to reach a conclusion they all agree on.

Life at Home

At the door to any Japanese home is a line of shoes. The Japanese often wear slippers inside their homes, to help keep them clean. Homes are often divided up by *shoji*, wooden frames covered in paper. The walls slide back when more open space is needed. In traditional homes, people eat at a low table, sitting on floor cushions rather than seats. At night they sleep on the floor on *futons*, mattresses, which are rolled up when they are not being used. Putting futons away during the day means that the sleeping area can be used for other activities. Futons are so comfortable that they have also become popular outside Japan.

In the past, Japanese grandparents, parents, and children used to all live in the same house. Children had to listen to their grandfather more than to their father. Respect for age is still important, but

▲ Even in modern apartments, families sit on cushions to eat at low tables.

▼ Tradition lives on in the geisha, a woman trained to sing, dance, and make pleasant conversation in order to entertain clients.

IT'S A GIFT

The Japanese often give gifts to their families, friends, and colleagues. At the end of the year, everyone gives gifts called *oseibo*, but gifts are given at other times of the year, too, to say "thank you." Subway stations have stores selling pre-wrapped gifts for people going to see friends.

The gifts are a sign of respect, so how they are presented is often more important than the actual gift. They must be carefully wrapped in gift paper or placed in a gift box. People do not usually open a gift in front of the giver, in case it is more or less valuable than the gift that has been given in return. Some gifts never get opened—people keep them to pass on when they next need to give a present.

most people now live in smaller family units of two parents and their children.

Growing Up

Most Japanese children go to school for 12 years. In high school, the students work hard to pass college exams. Many take extra classes after school. Some people complain that children are under so much pressure to do well that they suffer from stress. More than nine out of ten students graduate. They may go to junior college for two years or university for four years.

Young Japanese often socialize in groups of close friends, rather than dating members of the opposite sex. Some people still choose an arranged marriage, or *omiai*. A go-between suggests possible partners, but the couple still gets to choose whether or not to marry.

Most Japanese observe both Buddhism and the Shinto religion. Marriage services generally follow Shinto teaching, as do

▼ Japanese eat sushi with chopsticks— but they also use knives and forks for Western dishes.

THE ANCIENT TEA CEREMONY

Ceremonial tea drinking was brought to Japan by Zen Buddhist monks in the 1200s. They developed a simple but precise ceremony that is still followed today. The rules and rituals of Chanoyu ("the way of tea") emphasize simplicity. They use tea-drinking to encourage people to be calm and aware of beauty. The tea room should stand in a garden and be simple, small, and very clean. For decoration, it should have a scroll (*kakemono*) with calligraphy (elegant

▲ The tea ceremony is performed by experts who spend a long time learning the precise sequence of movements.

handwriting) or an ink painting, and an alcove with a flower arrangement. The tea for Chanoyu is thick and green. It is brewed over a charcoal fire and poured into large cups without handles. Tea drinkers stay quiet. They may have a short, formal conversation, but mainly they concentrate on the servers' movements, the beauty of their surroundings, and the taste of the tea.

coming of age ceremonies. Funerals, on the other hand, are more often Buddhist.

Japanese Food

Japanese food is very different from food in Western countries, with lots of rice, fish, and vegetables, but not much meat. Most Japanese used to eat rice at every meal, even for breakfast, where it was served in a soup with a salty paste called *miso*. It was so important that it was used as a measure of someone's wealth until the 1850s. Today, the word for cooked rice (*gohan*) also means "a meal."

The Japanese enjoy dishes of thinly sliced raw fish, known as *sashimi*, which is often eaten with rice. Chefs

▲ Young Kabuki actors in makeup play video games backstage during a performance.

cut the fish to bring out its flavors. Sashimi is too expensive to eat every day. So is *fugu*, but it is a great delicacy—for brave diners. The organs of this fish are poisonous, so the chef has to prepare it well. People die every year from eating fugu.

The best-known Japanese meal is *sushi*, clumps of vinegar-flavored rice with fillings or toppings of seafood or vegetables. Japanese also like to eat *tofu* (soybean curd). Commuters often eat a bowl of noodles standing at a stall in a railroad station.

With little fat or dairy and lots of vegetables, the traditional Japanese diet is very healthy. Japan has the longest life expectancy in the world. On average, men live to age 78 and women to age 85. But many Japanese also increasingly enjoy Western cooking— both in fancy restaurants and from fast-food outlets. As people adopt a Western diet, health problems such as heart disease are rising.

Theater and Music

Japan's traditional theater is different from any other. The Noh and Kabuki styles are renowned around the

MANGA AND ANIME

Comics and animated movies aren't just for children in Japan. They have many adult fans and deal with serious and sometimes violent subjects. Comic books are called *manga* in Japanese. Popular manga are made into films called *anime*, Japanese for "animation." Manga and anime mix traditional Japanese drawing with Western cartoon styles. The characters often have exaggerated hair and faces—and especially big eyes. Manga and anime are very important in Japanese popular culture. Manga magazines sell more copies in a week than American comic books sell in a year. The style of manga has inspired artists around the world.

▲ A commuter reads manga on the subway.

world. Noh theater developed in the 14th century from ancient Shinto dances. A performance involves only a few actors dressed in beautiful costumes, who use traditional poetry to tell ancient legends of gods, spirits, ghosts, warriors, and lovers. In Kabuki theater, all the parts are played by men. They wear brightly colored costumes and use special effects and more ordinary language to tell popular stories about city life.

Japan also has a distinctive form of cinema. The films of Akira Kurosawa are famous around the world. People say that

▼ Some young Japanese have adopted punk and grunge styles from the West.

NATIONAL HOLIDAYS

Japan's public holidays celebrate key events in the country's history, the yearly cycle of nature, and key stages in people's lives. The Emperor's Birthday holiday celebrates the emperor's actual birthday, so it moves when a new emperor comes to the throne.

JANUARY 1–3 New Year

JANUARY, SECOND MONDAY Coming of Age Day

FEBRUARY 11 National Foundation Day

MARCH 20 OR 21 Spring Equinox Day

APRIL 29 Showa Day

MAY 3 Constitution Memorial Day

MAY 4 Greenery Day

MAY 5 Children's Day

JULY, THIRD MONDAY Marine Day

SEPTEMBER 15 Respect for the Aged Day

SEPTEMBER 23 Autumn Equinox Day

OCTOBER, SECOND MONDAY Health and Sports Day

NOVEMBER 3 Culture Day

NOVEMBER 23 Labor Thanksgiving Day

DECEMBER 23 Emperor's Birthday

The Seven Samurai (1954) is one of the best movies ever made. It inspired the Hollywood western *The Magnificent Seven.*

The Japanese also love music. Some of it comes from the West: Japan has fine classical musicians and orchestras. Young Japanese enjoy the latest European and American pop music and they have their own versions of styles such as grunge and hip-hop (called "nip-hop"). There is also traditional music. *Gagaku* is used in Shinto ceremonies; *shomyo* is Buddhist chanting.

Karaoke, where people sing popular songs over recorded music, was invented in Kobe in the 1970s. The word means "empty orchestra." It has become popular around the world. Japanese cities have special bars where friends or colleagues can spend the evening singing karaoke.

Sports

Japan's national sport is sumo wrestling. It involves many rituals and is said to be entertainment for the

Shinto gods. Wrestlers weighing up to 440 pounds (200 kg) fight in a ring 15 feet (4.5 m) wide. A wrestler loses when he is pushed out of the ring or touches the ground with any part of his body apart from the soles of his feet.

Millions of Japanese take part in martial arts like judo, aikido, and karate. They are not only ways of fighting but also train a person's mind.

The Japanese also love foreign sports, such as soccer. The most popular is baseball. There are 12 professional teams in the country, and the standard is very high. Several Japanese players have played in the major leagues of the United States. Children also play the game, competing in high-school leagues.

▲ Sumo wrestlers wear their hair in a topknot, a traditional Japanese haircut.

▼ Soccer fans cheer the Japanese team in the 2002 World Cup.

The Miracle by Design

Paper umbrellas have been made in Japan since the 18th century, when craftsmen in the city of Gifu on Honshu were trying to recover from a devastating flood. They used local plants to make the paper, bamboo to make the frames, and sesame oil and lacquer for waterproofing. The industry soon took off. The umbrellas were both useful and beautiful to look at. The same principles shape Japan's industry today. The Japanese are famous for coming up with new products that are well designed and reliable. Clever innovation has transformed the economy from the devastation left by the end of World War II in 1945. Today Japan has the second largest economy in the world, after the United States. People call it a "miracle by design."

◀ **A woman makes traditional Japanese paper umbrellas. In addition to their high-tech economy, the Japanese still embrace their history and traditions.**

JAPAN'S LOCAL GOVERNMENT

Japan has 47 local government areas, known as prefectures or districts. Each has its own governor and assembly, both elected by local people. Prefectures vary in size and population. Tokyo is the largest. It contains more than 8 million people, some of whom live on the Ogasawara Islands, 1,200 miles (1,930 km) away. The smallest prefecture is Tottori in southwest Honshu. It is home to only 614,000 people.

Japan is also divided into eight regions. Regions have no role in government, but are often as important to people as their prefecture. People take great pride in their region's history and culture. From north to south, the regions are Hokkaido, Tohuku (northern Honshu), Kanto (eastern Honshu), Chubu (east-central Honshu), Kansai (west-central Honshu), Chugoku (western Honshu), Shikoku, and Kyushu, which also includes the Ryukyu Islands.

Trading Partners

Japan's most important trading partners are the United States, China, and other Pacific countries. It exports cars, computers and other electronic devices, and chemicals. It imports food, oil, and raw materials for its industry.

Country	Percentage of exports
United States	22.7%
European Union	15.8%
China	13.1%
South Korea	7.8%
Taiwan	7.4%
All others combined	33.2%

Country	Percentage of imports
China	20.7%
United States	14.0%
European Union	12.7%
South Korea	4.9%
Australia	4.3%
All others combined	43.4%

▲ Shinzo Abe, the Japanese prime minister, with U.S. secretary of state Condolezza Rice in 2005. Japan and the United States have been close allies since 1945.

128°E   130°E   132°E   134°E   136°E   138°E   140°E   142°E   144°E   146°E

RUSSIA

Sea of Okhotsk

46°N

Administered by Russia,
claimed by Japan

CHINA   RUSSIA

HOKKAIDO

42°N

Sapporo

NORTH
KOREA

MAP KEY

⊛   National capital

⊙   Prefecture capital

*Unlabeled prefectures bear the
names of their capitals*

Aomori

40°N

Morioka

OUTH
OREA

Akita   **IWATE**

0   miles   200

0   km   200

Sea
of
Japan

Yamagata   **MIYAGI**   Sendai

38°N

Niigata   Fukushima

**Pacific
Ocean**

UMBRELLA MAKER,
pages 3, 48-49

Nagano   **GUMMA**   Utsunomiya

Kanazawa Toyama   **TOCHIGI**   Mito

Fukui   Maebashi   **IBARAKI**

36°N

Saitama

Matsue   Tottori   Gifu   Kofu   Tokyo

Kyoto   Nagoya   **YAMANASHI**   Chiba

SHIMANE   Otsu   **AICHI**   Yokohama

HYOGO   Kobe   Nara   Tsu

Okayama   Osaka   **MIE**   Shizuoka

34°N

Hiroshima   **KAGAWA**   **TOKYO**

Yamaguchi   Matsuyama   Tokushima   Wakayama

Fukuoka   **EHIME**

Saga   Oita   Kochi

Nagasaki   WORKER'S RITUAL,
page 54
AND
ASSEMBLY LINE,
page 55

Kumamoto

DIPLOMATIC MEETING,
page 50
AND
STREET SCENE,
page 53
AND
ELECTRONICS DISPLAY,
page 55
AND
DISNEYLAND,
page 56

Takamatsu

32°N

Miyazaki

Kagoshima

0   mi   200

0   km   200

Kagoshima

Osumi Strait

ast
ina
ea

KAGOSHIMA

*Philippine
Sea*

CHINA

*East China
Sea*

KAGOSHIMA

TAIWAN   Naha

30°N

OKINAWA

*Philippine
Sea*

130°E   132°E   134°E   136°E   138°E   140°E   142°E   144°E

Political Map

The Emperor and Government

Japan is the only country in the world with a reigning emperor. In the past, the Japanese people believed that their emperor was a god. Before World War II, they owed him complete loyalty and were ready to die to defend him. Today, although they know he is human like them, Japanese still revere the emperor as a symbol of the country's traditions and unity.

When U.S. troops occupied Japan at the end of World War II in 1945, some people said that the position of emperor should be abolished. In the end, the position continued, but the emperor lost any real

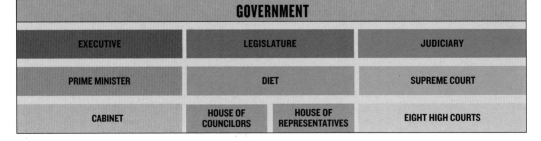

HOW THE GOVERNMENT WORKS

Japan is a constitutional monarchy. The emperor is the head of state, but the country is run by an elected government. The government is formed by members of the Diet, the Japanese parliament. The Diet is made up of two groups of politicians: the House of Representatives and the House of Councilors. Members of the two houses vote for a prime minister, who is then formally appointed by the emperor. The prime minister chooses members of the Cabinet. Each Cabinet minister has certain responsibilities, such as for the economy, education, or public health. The emperor appoints the chief judge of the Supreme Court, but the Cabinet appoints the other 14 Supreme Court judges. The judiciary (justice system) is independent of the rest of the government.

GOVERNMENT			
EXECUTIVE	LEGISLATURE		JUDICIARY
PRIME MINISTER	DIET		SUPREME COURT
CABINET	HOUSE OF COUNCILORS	HOUSE OF REPRESENTATIVES	EIGHT HIGH COURTS

power. He has only ceremonial duties. Emperor Hirohito inspired the Japanese as they set about rebuilding their country.

In 1989, Emperor Akihito became the 125th Japanese emperor. Emperors were traditionally seldom seen by their people, but Akihito followed his father in making frequent contact with them. He has set out to improve Japan's relations with its neighbors, celebrating its ancient links with Korea, for example.

Japan is governed by a prime minister nominated by the Diet, or parliament. Members of the Diet are elected by the public; everyone over age 20 can vote. Japanese politics are very stable. The Liberal Democratic Party (LDP) has been in power almost without a break since 1955. In 2006, the prime minister was Shinzo Abe.

Economic Miracle

After Japan regained independence in 1952, the country began to build a modern economy. It was a great challenge.

▲ Japan's lively cities reflect its economic growth since 1945.

▼ Sony, which built this robot dog, is one of Japan's leading firms.

COMPANY CULTURE

▲ Workers in an auto plant perform a ritual before work.

Until recently, most Japanese workers worked for the same company for their whole careers. They showed great loyalty to the company, which in return promised to promote them according to their length of service. In some cases, that meant that workers were promoted even if they were not good at their jobs. For some people, the culture of lifetime employment still exists. In certain industries, workers take part in daily exercise programs. They also socialize with the people they work with, for example before New Year company parties called *bonenkai*. However, for many Japanese, life has changed since the 1990s, when Japan's economy struggled. Firms could no longer offer lifetime employment or automatic promotion. Today, people are more willing and able to move between jobs. The job for life still exists—but it is increasingly a thing of the past.

Half of Japanese workers worked in agriculture, and most of their produce was not sold abroad. Japan also had few natural resources, such as oil or iron. They had to be imported in order to make goods for export. The Japanese concentrated on developing new products and making their factories efficient to keep their costs low. By the 1960s, Japan had become known for making ships, cars, and electronic goods—including portable radios, a new invention at the time.

In the 1970s, the price of oil rose around the world. Countries such as Japan could not as easily afford the fuel needed for their industry. Japanese businesses became more efficient at using energy.

They also began making more cars, computers, TVs, personal stereos, and other electronic goods to export. Small and economical Japanese cars sold well, and makes such as Toyota and Honda became popular worldwide.

In the 1990s economic growth ended. Other countries became more efficient at producing similar goods. The value of Japanese companies fell rapidly. The economy began to recover in 2003, however.

Trading Giant

Japan's economy makes it very important in the modern world. Its high-tech industry has a reputation for making useful products that are the best of their type. Japanese companies such as Sony, Panasonic, Toyota, and Nikon are known and admired around the world. Their cutting-edge products find enthusiastic customers everywhere.

Many of those customers are in the West. Since World War II, Japan and the United States have had particularly strong trading links. Japan sends more than 20 percent of its exports to America. In 2005, these were worth $138 billion. Japan is the fourth most important market for U.S. exports, after Canada, the European Union, and Mexico. In 2005, the United States exported $55 billion worth of products to Japan.

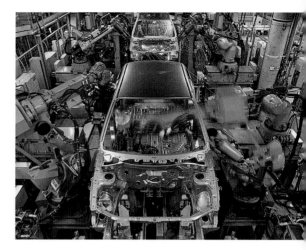

▲ Automated assembly lines like this Mazda auto plant cut costs—and reduced the need for workers.

▼ Young shoppers love to be right up to the minute with the latest technology, like these cell phones in Tokyo.

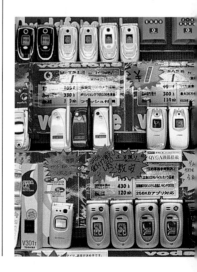

INDUSTRIAL JAPAN

This map shows the industrial areas of Japan. The most important industrial region is in eastern Honshu around the capital city of Tokyo.

MAP KEY

Major Mines
Au Gold
C Coal
Cu Copper
Pb Lead
Zn Zinc

⚙ Manufacturing center
Cu Processing plant
Steel Steel manufacturing

Sea of Japan

Pacific Ocean

C C
Pb Zn

Pb
Cu

Cu
Nagoya
Pb
Kyoto
Cu
Kobe
Cu
Hiroshima
Cu
Osaka
Kitakyushu
Fukuoka
Cu
Nagasaki
Cu
Au
Hamamatsu
Wakayama
Steel
Steel
Tokyo
Yokohama

0   mi   200
0   km 200

The Past and the Future

As well as large companies that export modern goods around the world, Japan still has many small workshops. They manufacture traditional products, such as ornamental pots and silk clothes, or make supplies for the large companies.

Tourism is increasingly important. Although it is expensive for visitors to travel around Japan, the beautiful landscape and historical sites are a great attraction. The Japanese make the most of their long history. Many old buildings have been turned into luxury inns called *ryokans*. Guests enjoy traditions such as bathing in *ofuro*, deep wooden baths,

▶ Japanese are eager to experience foreign culture as well as their own. Tokyo Disneyland, which opened in 1983, was the first to be built outside of the United States.

before eating dinner in traditional robes and sleeping on futons. There are also fascinating local and national festivals, often incorporating colorful Shinto processions or Buddhist traditions. In addition, visitors feel very safe in Japan. The country has one of the lowest crime rates in the world.

A Country at Ease

The Japanese take great pride in their modern achievements. However, they are also proud of their religious and artistic history, their culture, and the great natural beauty of their country. They appreciate the importance both of their traditions, such as the tea ceremony, and their new technology, such as the bullet train. They admire both the traditional arts of origami paper-folding or flower arranging (*ikebana*) and the high-tech design of the newest digital camera or cell phone. They see the successful combination of the past and the present as an example to the rest of the world.

LIKE A BULLET

The *shinkansen*, which was also known as the bullet train, was the world's first high-speed train when it was introduced in 1964 at the time the Olympic Games were held in Tokyo. It was named for its high speeds. The train became a symbol of how successfully Japan had rebuilt itself as a forward-looking economy. The train travels at up to 185 miles per hour (300 km/h) and was the world's fastest passenger train until 1990, when the French TGV was launched. Express shinkansen services link Tokyo to many of the main cities on Honshu and Kyushu islands.

▲ Old and new in harmony: A geisha waits for her bullet train to depart.

Add a Little Extra to Your Country Report!

I f you are assigned to write a report about Japan, you'll want to include basic information about the country, of course. The Fast Facts chart on page 8 will give you a good start. The rest of the book will give you the details you need to create a full and up-to-date paper or PowerPoint presentation. But what can you do to make your report more fun than anyone else's? If you use your imagination and dig a bit deeper into some of the topics introduced in this book, you're sure to come up with information that will make your report unique!

>Flag

Perhaps you could explain the history of Japan's flag, and the meanings of its colors and symbols. Go to **www.crwflags.com/fotw/flags** for more information.

>National Anthem

How about downloading Japan's national anthem and playing it for your class? At **www.nationalanthems.info** you'll find what you need, including the words to the anthem in Japanese and English, plus sheet music for the anthem. Simply pick "J" and then "Japan" from the list on the left-hand side of the screen, and you're on your way.

>Time Difference

If you want to understand the time difference between Japan and where you are, this Web site can help: **www.worldtimeserver.com**. Just select "Current Times" and then pick "Japan" from the list on the right. If you called Japan right now, would you wake whomever you are calling?

>Currency

Another Web site will convert your money into yen, the currency used in Japan. You'll want to know how much money to bring if you're ever lucky enough to travel to Japan: **www.xe.com/ucc**.

>Weather

Why not check the current weather in Japan? It's easy—simply go to **www.weather.com** to find out if it's sunny or cloudy, warm or cold in a particular place in Japan right this minute! Enter the name of a Japanese city in the search box at the top of the page and click "Go." Be sure to click on the tabs below the weather report for Sunrise/Sunset information, Weather Watch, and Business Travel Outlook, too. Scroll down the page for the 36-hour Forecast and a satellite weather map. Compare your weather to the weather in the Japanese city you chose. Is this a good season, weather-wise, for a person to travel to Japan?

>Miscellaneous

Still want more information? Simply go to National Geographic's One-Stop Research site at **http://www.nationalgeographic.com/onestop**. It will help you find maps, photos and art, articles and information, games, and features that you can use to jazz up your report.

Glossary

Archipelago a scattered group of islands.

Atomic bomb a bomb that uses chemical changes in atoms to trigger an explosion far stronger than ordinary explosives.

Baptism a religious ceremony held to mark the naming of a child.

Bonsai the art of pruning and shaping regular trees to create dwarf versions.

Buddhist a person who follows the teachings of Buddhism.

Bullet train a high-speed train with a front shaped like a bullet to enable it to pass smoothly through the air.

Bushido Japanese for "the way of the warrior"; a set of rules of behavior for samurai and other Japanese troops.

Clan a family or group of people descended from the same ancestor.

Commuter someone who travels to and from work every day, often from a suburb into a city.

Constitution a document that lays out laws about how a country should be governed.

Current a steady stream of water within the ocean.

Endangered species an animal or plant that is at risk of dying out.

Geisha a girl or woman trained to provide entertaining and amusing company, usually for a man or group of men.

Judo a sport in which opponents try to throw one another to the floor.

Karate a sport in which opponents strike one another with their hands and feet.

Lacquer a hard varnish for wood that is built up in layers to create a decorative effect.

Origami the art of folding paper to create objects and shapes.

Peninsula land that is nearly surrounded by water.

Plate one of the large sections that make up the surface of the Earth.

Prefecture an area of a country that is partly run by a local government, like a state.

Reenactment the re-creation of a historic event for entertainment.

Shrine a place where people honor a god, goddess, or other holy being.

Species a type of organism; animals or plants in the same species look similar and can only breed successfully among themselves.

Subtropical describing a region that lies outside the tropics but has a similar hot and wet climate.

Suspension bridge a bridge whose deck is held up by cables, usually supported by towers.

Trade agreement an arrangement between countries that reduces obstacles to trade, such as high taxes on imports or exports.

Tropical lying in a wide band around the middle of the Earth north or south of the equator.

Tsunami a tidal wave caused by an earthquake beneath the seabed.

Warlord a leader who gains local power by commanding his own military force.

Wet paddy a field flooded with shallow water in which rice is grown.

Bibliography

Bowring, Richard, and Peter Kornicki (eds). *Cambridge Encyclopedia of Japan*. New York: Cambridge University Press, 1993.

Gordon, Andrew. *Modern History of Japan*. New York:

Oxford University Press, 2003.

http://jguide.stanford.edu/ (Virtual Guide to Japan at Stanford University)

http://web-japan.org/index.html (Gateway sponsored by

Japan's Ministry of Foreign Affairs)

http://lcweb2.loc.gov/frd/cs/ jptoc.html (Country Guide at the Library of Congress)

Further Information

NATIONAL GEOGRAPHIC Articles

Ackerman, Jennifer. "When the Frost Lies White: Japan's Winter Wildlife." NATIONAL GEOGRAPHIC (January 2003): 88–113.

Bellows, Keith. "The Zen of Kyoto." NATIONAL GEOGRAPHIC TRAVELER (March 2005): 78–88.

Buettner, Dan. "The Secrets of Long Life." NATIONAL GEOGRAPHIC (November 2005): 2–27.

Dahlby, Tracy. "Tokyo Bay." NATIONAL GEOGRAPHIC (October 2002): 32–57.

Earnhart, Stephen. "Japan's Backcountry Dojo." NATIONAL GEOGRAPHIC ADVENTURE (February 2006): 18–21.

Eliot, John. "Jelly Giant." NATIONAL GEOGRAPHIC (August 2006): Wildlife.

Gup, Ted. "Up from Ground Zero: Hiroshima." NATIONAL GEOGRAPHIC (August 1995): 78–101.

Karnow, Catherine. "Showdown in Sumo Town." NATIONAL GEOGRAPHIC TRAVELER (July/August 2004): 114.

Kiffel, Jamie. "The Legend of the Samurai." NATIONAL GEOGRAPHIC KIDS (January/February 2004): 30–31.

O'Neill, Tom. "Samurai: Japan's Way of the Warrior." NATIONAL GEOGRAPHIC (December 2003): 98–131.

Web sites to explore

More fast facts about Japan, from the CIA (Central Intelligence Agency): https://www.cia.gov/cia /publications/factbook/geos /ja.html

Japan National Tourist Organization—remember to click "English"! http://www.jnto.go.jp/

Want to know more about Japanese music? The University of Texas can tell you all about it: http://inic.utexas.edu/asnic/co untries/japan/japmusic.html

Concerned about wildlife in Japan? So is the Japan Wildlife Conservation Society: http://www.jwcs.org/english /index.html

Want to hear some Japanese phrases and see loads of cool stuff just for kids?: http://web-japan.org/kidsweb /index.html

Index

Credits

Picture Credits

Front Cover—Spine: Sisse Brimberg/NG Image Collection; Top: Justin Guariglia/NG Image Collection; Low far left: Darlyne A. Murawski/NG Image Collection; Low left: Michael S. Yamashita/NG Image Collection; Low right: Paul Chesley/NG Image Collection; Low far right: Karen Kasmauski/NG Image Collection.

Interior—Corbis: Bettmann: 33 up; Michael S. Yamashita: 20 lo, 22 up; Burstein Collection: 22 lo; Yuri Gripas: 50 lo; Reuters: 35 lo; Roger Ressmeyer: 45 lo; Gregor Schaster: 59 up; Maurat Taner: 12 center; NG Image Collection: 32 up; Sam Abell: 2 right, 16–17; Ira Block: 31 up, 31 lo; Sisse Brimberg: 3 right, 48–49; Paul Chesley: 13 lo, 38 center, 57 lo; Jodi Cobb: 34 lo, 40 center, 47 lo, 54 up, 55 up; Robert Clark: 53 lo; David Alan Harvey: 41 up; Karen Kasmauski: 11 lo, 13 up, 15 center, 35 up; Kenneth Garrett: 26 center; Justin Guariglia: TP, 3 left, 41 lo, 45 up, 53 up, 55 lo; Tim Laman: 21 up; George F. Mobley: 28 up, 36–37; Darlyne A. Murawski: 42 lo; Richard Nowtiz: 2 left, 6–7; Nicholas Reynard: 47 up; Michael S. Yamashita: 2–3, 5 up, 10 lo, 11 up, 14 center, 18 lo, 24–25, 29 lo, 30 center, 43 up, 44 up, 56 lo.

Text copyright © 2007 National Geographic Society
Published by the National Geographic Society.
All rights reserved. Reproduction of the whole or any part of the contents without written permission from the National Geographic Society is strictly prohibited. For information about special discounts for bulk purchases, contact National Geographic Special Sales: ngspecsales@ngs.org

For more information, please call 1-800-NGS-LINE (647-5463) or write to the following address:

NATIONAL GEOGRAPHIC SOCIETY
1145 17th Street N.W.
Washington, D.C. 20036-4688 U.S.A.

Visit the Society's Web site at www.nationalgeographic.com

Library of Congress Cataloging-in-Publication Data available on request
ISBN: 978-1-4263-0029-5

Printed in the United States of America

Series design by Jim Hiscott.
The body text is set in Avenir; Knockout.
The display text is set in Matrix Script.

Front Cover—Top: Pedestrians cross a Tokyo street at night; Low Far Left: Cherry blossoms; Low Left: A priest rakes a gravel garden at a Zen Buddhist temple in Kyoto; Low Right: A geisha performs a traditional dance with a folding fan; Low Far Right: A view of Mt. Fuji through clouds

Page 1—Colleagues greet each other on a street in a business district in Tokyo; Icon image on spine, Contents page, and throughout: A scowling warrior from a Japanese paper kite

Produced through the worldwide resources of the National Geographic Society

John M. Fahey, Jr., *President and Chief Executive Officer*; Gilbert M. Grosvenor, *Chairman of the Board*; Nina D. Hoffman, *Executive Vice President, President of Book Publishing Group*

National Geographic Staff for this Book

Nancy Laties Feresten, *Vice President, Editor-in-Chief of Children's Books*
Bea Jackson, *Director of Design and Illustration*
Virginia Koeth, *Project Editor*
Lori Epstein, *Illustrations Editor*
Stacy Gold, Nadia Hughes *Illustrations Research Editors*
Carl Mehler, *Director of Maps*
Priyanka Lamichhane, *Assistant Editor*
R. Gary Colbert, *Production Director*
Lewis R. Bassford, *Production Manager*
Maryclare Tracy, Nicole Elliott, *Manufacturing Managers*

Brown Reference Group plc. Staff for this Book

Volume Editor: Tom Jackson
Designer: Dave Allen
Picture Manager: Becky Cox
Maps: Martin Darlinson
Artwork: Darren Awuah
Index: Kay Ollerenshaw
Senior Managing Editor: Tim Cooke
Design Manager: Sarah Williams
Children's Publisher: Anne O'Daly
Editorial Director: Lindsey Lowe

About the Author

CHARLES PHILLIPS has written more than 20 books, mainly about history, archaeology, and myth. He lives in London with his young family. This is his first book for NATIONAL GEOGRAPHIC.

About the Consultants

GIL LATZ is vice provost for international affairs and professor of geography at Portland State University, Portland, Oregon. His research focuses on the political and economic geography of Japan. Dr. Latz's most recent work is as co-editor, with Gerald Curtis and Masato Kimura, of *Nihon no Chosen* (Challenges for Japan), 2006. He is an editor for the journal *Asian Perspective*, and co-host for the Corporation for Public Broadcasting's *Teaching Geography*, 2002.

KYOHEI SHIBATA is a professor at Shinshu University, Nagano Prefecture, Japan. Born and raised in Akita Prefecture, he received a bachelor's degree of liberal arts and sciences from the University of Tokyo. He has taught regional issues of Pacific Asia and Japan at Portland State University, Oregon. He has participated in several translation projects in the field of geography, including the *Oxford Dictionary of Geography*. He currently serves as the dean of the Faculty of Economics of Shinshu University.

Time Line of
Japanese History

B.C.

2000 The Jomon culture reaches its peak and begins to create group burial mounds.

660 According to legend, Jimmu Tenno, a descendent of the sun goddess Amaterasu Omikami, takes control of Japan and becomes its first emperor.

300 The Yayoi, Japan's first entirely agricultural people, expand throughout the country and take control from the Jomon.

A.D.

ca 350 Japan becomes unified under an emperor.

ca 400 The Yamato become the most powerful clan in Japan.

552 The Buddhist religion arrives from China.

710 Heijo (also known as Nara) becomes Japan's first permanent capital. The city's gridded streets are similar to those of Chang'an, the Chinese capital during the Tang dynasty.

794 The Heian period begins and the capital moves to Heian-kyo, present-day Kyoto. The city remains the capital until 1868.

1000

ca 1000 Lady Murasaki, an upper-class lady-in-waiting, writes *The Tale of Genji*. The book is the world's first novel.

1100

1192 Emperor Go-Toba names Minamoto Yoritomo shogun, or military commander. The appointment establishes a political system in which the emperor is a figurehead and shoguns rule the country.

1500

1543 Portuguese sailors land on Tanegashima Island and make the first contact between Europeans and Japanese.

1600

1639 The shogunate closes Japan to Western influence by expelling all European residents.

1800

1823 Katsushika Hokusai produces his best-selling series of woodblock prints called *Thirty-six Views of Mount Fuji*, which includes a popular image of fishers sailing into a wave.

1853 Commodore Matthew Perry arrives in Edo Bay and requests that Japan make trade agreements with the United States.

1858 The Harris Treaty allows American and European traders into Japanese ports. It gives the United States "most favored nation" status, which angers some Japanese.

1868 Emperor Mutsuhito comes to the throne, beginning the Meiji Restoration.